# The Adventures of Little Mousey

Catherine Santamera

AuthorHouse™ UK Ltd.
1663 Liberty Drive
Bloomington, IN 47403 USA
www.authorhouse.co.uk
Phone: 0800.197.4150

Interior Graphics/Art Credit : THOMAS DONAHUE

Published by AuthorHouse 12/28/2013

ISBN: 978-1-4918-8817-9 (sc)
ISBN: 978-1-4918-8850-6 (e)

This book is printed on acid-free paper.

authorHOUSE®

The Adventures of Little Mousey

For darling Lily Pie
The apple of Grandmas
Eye

This book belongs to:

_____

Little Mousey lived in a big barn in the countryside. He had lots of brothers and sisters, and they had lots of fun together playing hide and seek amongst the bales of hay that were stored in the barn.

One day, Little Mousey heard a commotion outside the barn. He could hear horses' hooves clattering on the stone floor of the yard and a man's deep voice saying, "Whoa, Girl! Whoa, Christy!"

Little Mousey scampered down the haystacks to see what was going on. When he got outside in the yard, he saw a man in a green coat and flat cap leading two young fell ponies to their feed trough on the wall of the barn. It was stuffed full of sweet-smelling new hay. Christy was the biggest pony. He was five years old – one year older than his sister, Star, who was four. Her name was Star because she had a white star-shaped blaze on her forehead. It looked very cute peeping through her forelock when she shook her head, and she was shaking it now because she was cross with Christy, who was scoffing up all the hay, as usual.

"Give Star a chance, Christy!" said the man with the deep voice.

Little Mousey was very careful when he was near the ponies' hooves so that they wouldn't step on him. So he clambered into an empty watering can which was hanging nearby. Just then he heard a cat calling, "Meow! Meow!" Little Mousey climbed up into the haystacks, then went higher still up to the big beam that was in the barn's roof. He snuggled into a large spiderweb that Belinda Spider had made and settled in for a nice sleep. He was so warm and comfy that soon he began to snore softly.

All at once he awoke to another commotion below him in the barn. Again, he heard the cat loudly say, "Meow!" Little Mousey did not like cats. He had been told that they find small mice very tasty and that he should stay away from them. Sometimes this cat climbed up into the haystacks and sniffed around for mice. Little Mousey carefully peeped over the edge of the beam to see what was happening below him. What he saw shocked him so badly, he almost fell. The cat was big, fierce-looking, and black and white. He chased and caught one of Little Mousey's brothers. Little Mousey went stiff with fright as the cat pounced on Sammy, his little brother.

The cat screeched, "Meow!"

Poor Sammy squealed, "Help me!"

Little Mousey wondered what on earth he could do to help Sammy. Then, just as the cat looked like he was ready to eat Sammy all up, Little Mousey saw the pile of nuts at the end of the beam. He very slowly and carefully crept along to the nuts and pushed them off one by one. The nuts fell from the beam down to the haystack and landed beside the cat with a plop, plop, plop. This startled the cat so much that it let go of Sammy, who was able to get free and run away to the barn floor. Little Mousey clung to the beam and watched in fear and astonishment as the dreadful cat gave chase and caught Sammy again! Sammy squeaked in terror as the cat, using his fat paws with their sharp claws extended, pounced on his tail.

Sammy bravely struggled to get away. The nasty cat hit Sammy across his nose with his left paw, which made poor Sammy very dizzy. The cat hit him again with his right paw. As Sammy struggled to get away, he became even dizzier. And so it went on and on. First a right slap, then a left slap, over and over, again and again. The cat and mouse ran around this way and that for what seemed to Little Mousey to be a very long time.

Little Mousey was feeling quite dizzy just from watching the whole sorry episode unfold below him. He began to think Sammy would never get away when just in the nick of time, help arrived in the shape of an old blue tractor, which came hissing and phut-phut-phutting its way noisily into the barn. This scared the cat and its tail stood up in the air. Sammy escaped as the cat ran away in fright.

High up on the beam, Little Mousey breathed a big sigh of relief and ran down the haystacks to find Sammy and comfort him. Sammy was very pleased with Little Mousey.

"Thank you! Thank you so much, Little Mousey," Sammy gasped. He was breathless from his terrifying ordeal.

Little Mousey gave Sammy a reassuring hug and Sammy snuggled into it, happy his ordeal was now over and the cat had gone. Sammy scampered happily up the haystacks to find his other brothers and sisters and tell them what had happened. Although Little Mousey was thrilled to have saved Sammy from that fierce black-and-white cat, he now began to worry that he might be in trouble for losing their winter store of nuts. It had taken the mice a very long time and lots of hard work to gather the nuts and carry them from the orchard nearby, across to the barn, and up over the haystacks onto the beam high in the barn roof. But he needn't have worried, because when Sammy explained to everybody that Little Mousey used the nuts to save him from that nasty cat, everyone jumped up and down with glee and sang at the top of their voices, "For he's a jolly good fellow! For he's a jolly good fellow! For he's a jolly good fe-l-l-low! And so say all of us! And so say all of us!"

Sammy, Little Mousey, and all of their brothers and sisters celebrated by playing and singing on the haystacks until it became dark and they were very, very sleepy. Finally, when the moon came out, Sammy and Mousey snuggled up together on another of Belinda Spider's cobwebs and fell fast asleep.

The next morning while Sammy was still sleeping, he felt something quite gentle tickle his whiskers. It made him squeal with surprise, and this woke Little Mousey. "It's okay, Sammy," he said. "It's just Belinda Spider busy making her cobwebs."

"Oh dear. Did I wake you? It is late morning, you know, and the sun is high in the sky," said Belinda disdainfully.

Sammy stretched himself and yawned. "It's a nice day today, Mousey. Shall we go and pick some blackberries?"

Mousey stretched himself awake as he thought about Sammy's suggestion. He loved blackberries. They were so juicy and sweet, and he knew there were lots and lots of them in the bramble bushes that bordered the orchard. "Yes, Sammy, that's a great idea. Let's go now while the sun is shining."

"Yes, let's," said Sammy, and they both scampered from the beam down to the haystacks below and out of the barn into the yard.

They looked about carefully, noses twitching nervously in case that dreadful cat was lurking somewhere. But, with no sign of the cat, they quickly ran across the yard to the orchard. Belinda smiled to herself as she watched them go and remained on the beam busily making some large cobwebs so the little mice would have somewhere nice and soft to lie down and have a nap after they had filled their hungry little tummies with blackberries.

When Mousey and Sammy reached the blackberry bush, they could hear little girls giggling and talking to each other. "Oh, Mimi, these blackberries are scrummy scrumptious!" said Lily.

Mimi giggled. "Yes, they're delicious, but," she chuckled between mouthfuls of juicy berries, "you've got a purple moustache from the berry juice!"

"So have you!" Lily chuckled. "Watch out and don't wipe your fingers on your t-shirt. It will stain with the juice on your fingers."

Lily popped another juicy blackberry into her mouth just as Mimi nudged her with her elbow. "Look, Lily," she whispered. "Cute little mice eating blackberries just like you and me."

The girls stood quietly licking their lips and watching Sammy and Little Mousey devouring the juicy blackberries. Lily popped some more blackberries into her mouth, and Mimi nudged her gently again with her elbow and said, with her own mouth full of the juicy berries, "You're not supposed to eat them all you know! Put some in the basket so your grandma can make some of her delicious blackberry jam."

Lily giggled and said, "Look, Mimi, even the little mouse has a purple nose from eating the berries!" Both girls giggled as they continued picking blackberries. They disturbed the branch Sammy and Little Mousey were clinging to, so both mice scampered away across the orchard and back to the barn.

As they nestled into the cobwebs that Belinda had made, Sammy said, "Lily was right you know."

"Who?" asked Mousey.

"The little girl picking blackberries. She said you had a purple nose."

"So do you, Sammy," said Little Mousey."

"We know where you two have been," called their brothers and sisters. "The blackberries have stained your noses and whiskers purple!"

Happy and content after a busy sunny day feasting on blackberries, Sammy and Mousey cuddled into their soft bed of cobwebs and quickly dozed off to sleep. Mousey was almost asleep when Sammy whispered, "Hey, Mousey, what is jam?"

"Go to sleep, Sammy. I am too sleepy for chatting now. But I think it is sticky gooey stuff made from sugar and fruit."

"It sounds delicious," said Sammy.

"Oh, please go to sleep, Sammy!"

"Goodnight, Mousey," groaned Sammy, who wanted to have a chat about their day. After a few minutes, all Mousey could hear was the sound of Sammy's soft snoring. Zzzzzzzzzz.

A few minutes later, Little Mousey was also fast asleep and snoring softly. Zzzzzzzzzz.

Lightning Source UK Ltd.
Milton Keynes UK
UKIC01n0607180214
226652UK00002B/23